Where's Rudolph?

Find Rudolph and his festive helpers in 15 fun-filled puzzles

Written by Danielle James
Illustrated by Dan Green
Design by Graeme Andrew

JB

JOHN BLAKE

Published by John Blake Publishing Ltd,
3 Bramber Court, 2 Bramber Road,
London W14 9PB, England

www.johnblakepublishing.co.uk

www.facebook.com/johnblakebooks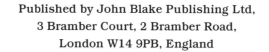
twitter.com/jblakebooks

First published in hardback in 2014

ISBN: 978 1 78418 016 4

British Library Cataloguing-in-Publication Data:

A catalogue record for this book is available from the British Library.

Printed and bound in Italy by L.E.G.O. S.p.A

1 3 5 7 9 10 8 6 4 2

Papers used by John Blake Publishing are natural, recyclable products made from wood grown in sustainable forests. The manufacturing processes conform to the environmental regulations of the country of origin.

Every attempt has been made to contact the relevant copyright-holders, but some were unobtainable. We would be grateful if the appropriate people could contact us.

Ho ho ho, Merry Christmas!

My name is Father Christmas, but I'm sure you knew that already! I live in Lapland with Mrs Christmas and thousands of festive helpers. We spend all year preparing for Christmas day, one of the happiest days of the year. I have a team of penguins, a team of snowmen, a team of elves, a team of robins and a team of reindeer to help me organise the big day. Every year I pick someone to be in charge of the different teams. This year, Noelle is helping the elves to make the toys, Marvin is instructing the robins to deliver my post, Blue is teaching the snowmen to bake and Rocky is looking for the perfect tree with the other penguins. Lastly, I have asked Rudolph to guide my sleigh, which is a very important task. We were busy last year, because there were so many good girls and boys, so this year I needed someone who I could rely on to guide the other reindeer and help me deliver the presents. Rudolph also took part in the reindeer training school and excelled himself. He's the best reindeer in the world, and that's why I have asked him to be my second in command! This year, he will be training the new recruits so that I will have the best team guiding my sleigh.

Rudolph is really looking forward to meeting you. I think you will have lots of fun with him and my other helpers, just make sure you stay on your best behaviour – I want to make sure all the presents are delivered on time.

Love Father Christmas

I am so excited and can't wait to tell you all my news! Last year I was part of Father Christmas's elite flying squad and, after taking part in the reindeer training school, this year I have been chosen to lead the reindeers on Christmas day. But, that's not all – I am going to be Father Christmas's second in command, which means that I have to oversee the whole Christmas team. Christmas is a big operation, so I'm thrilled that Rocky, Noelle, Blue and Marvin are helping me – they are my best friends, too, so there will be plenty of laughs! We have so much to do before Christmas Eve, including shopping for food, making toys, answering mail, baking mince pies and

selecting the tree, but there's plenty of fun to be had, too. I love ice skating and skiing in my spare time, even on my four legs, and December is the perfect time to get my skates on. I'm so happy you are going to be helping me this year! I'm going to need you, especially because my friends can be mischievous. Sometimes they hide from me, so you're going to have to help me find them if they go missing.

We're almost ready to begin our adventure, so have your wits about you and prepare to have the time of your life, but first you must say hello to my friends!

Rudolph

Rudolph's Helpers

Find out more about Rudolph's friends and discover what they look like. It will help you find them quicker if they do go missing!

Noelle

Noelle is Father Christmas's number one Elf this year. Her father, Jingle, worked for Father Christmas for many, many years, so she's very happy to be following in his footsteps. Throughout the year, she has helped Father Christmas sort out the mail, keep a close eye on the girls and boys, and organise the decorations. There's not much left on her 'to do' list, but one of the most important tasks left is to instruct the other elves on how to make the best Christmas presents, before loading them all onto the sleigh. She can't wait to start making the toys because it's her favourite thing to do!

LIKES: Making presents
DISLIKES: Oranges
FAVOURITE SONG: 'Jingle Bells'
FAVOURITE FOOD: Mince Pies

Marvin

Marvin is only small but he is a very important part of Father Christmas's festive team. Marvin is responsible for delivering the letters to Father Christmas's post office, and flying the replies back to the girls and boys. While he is delivering the post, he also checks to see who is being naughty and who is being nice. He keeps a note and lets Father Christmas know what he has seen! Marvin is really pleased to meet you and he knows by the end of the journey you will be best of friends!

LIKES: Letters
DISLIKES: Sticky tape
FAVOURITE SONG: 'Little Donkey'
FAVOURITE FOOD: Pine nuts

Blue

Blue loves the snow! He lives in an igloo next to the forest, and his neighbour is Rocky. Blue spends all day building snowballs or skiing with Rocky. Sometimes he plays tricks on his friend by hiding in the forest and throwing snowballs at him. Even though Blue is a mischievous snowman, Father Christmas trusts him to make the best mince pies and to find the perfect Christmas tree for the workshop.

LIKES: Icicles
DISLIKES: Fire
FAVOURITE SONG: 'Walking in the Air'
FAVOURITE FOOD: Turkey

Rocky

Friendly Rocky is always busy talking to the other penguins and everyone likes him, although sometimes he doesn't stop talking and Father Christmas has to tell him off. He loves showing Blue how to ski, but he also loves ice-skating. He's been practising since he was a baby penguin! When he isn't skiing, talking or skating, Rocky can be found hanging out with Father Christmas helping to organise the other penguins.

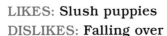

LIKES: Slush puppies
DISLIKES: Falling over
FAVOURITE SONG: 'All I Want For Christmas'
FAVOURITE FOOD: Fish

Father Christmas

Me again! I'm so happy you have decided to join us. I've just finished writing my 'to do' list and there are lots of things you can help me do. The most important thing will be to help me keep an eye on Rudolph, Rocky, Marvin, Noelle and Blue because sometimes they go missing! You probably should also know that while I am looking for them, sometimes I get lost, so you'll have to keep your eyes peeled for me too!

LIKES: Good girls and boys
DISLIKES: Naughty girls and boys
FAVOURITE SONG: 'Santa Claus'
FAVOURITE FOOD: Christmas cake

Toyshop

With more good girls and boys than ever, the elves are soon going to be busy working in their workshop, but first they must go shopping to see what presents they can make and what they need to buy. Everyone was excited looking at all the shiny new toys, and now Rudolph and his helpers are lost! Can you find them amongst the toys?

- [ ] A moneybox
- [ ] A blue scarf
- [ ] A dog wearing a ribbon
- [ ] A robot
- [ ] Pink shoes
- [ ] A goldfish
- [ ] A green snake
- [ ] A pigeon
- [ ] Green gloves
- [ ] A TV

BRAND NEW CARS

Princess Castle

Dolly

Mail Mania

Uh-oh, it looks as though Marvin has delivered thousands of letters to the Post Office and now the elves and robins are struggling to keep up! Rudolph and his friend have been caught up in all the commotion. Help the elves and robins in the sorting office to find their friends!

- [ ] A map of the world
- [ ] A telephone
- [ ] An elf in a yellow suit
- [ ] A feather
- [ ] A polka dot postbag
- [ ] A red balloon
- [ ] A polar bear
- [ ] A fishing rod
- [ ] Blue socks
- [ ] A pocket watch

Tree Maze

Now the mail has been sorted, the next task on Rudolph's list is to organise the shopping trip to the tree market. Rudolph knows that they will need a big tree to fill the workshop, and they'll also need hundreds of baubles and lights to make the tree look beautiful. The market is in full swing and everyone is getting in the festive spirit, but it's so busy that is has almost become a maze! Can you find everyone?

- [ ] A red tree
- [ ] 10 candy canes
- [ ] A husky dog
- [ ] A clown
- [ ] A horse and cart
- [ ] A pair of slippers
- [ ] A penguin singing
- [ ] A bow tie
- [ ] 10 stars
- [ ] A candle

A Christmas Carol

Rudolph and his friends have had a very busy few days shopping and posting mail, so Father Christmas has said they can have the day off to sing some Christmas carols. Blue loves singing and people have come from everywhere to hear. Rudolph was so excited to see old friends that he got lost amongst the crowds. Can you help find him and his friends?

- [ ] A pear tree
- [ ] 12 drummers drumming
- [ ] A penguin dancing
- [ ] A Christmas cracker
- [ ] Red and blue striped socks
- [ ] A football
- [ ] 7 swans
- [ ] A green hat
- [ ] 5 gold rings
- [ ] A bell

420

Supermarket Madness

It's back to work for Rudolph, Father Christmas, Rocky, Blue, Marvin and Noelle. Father Christmas likes to make sure he has enough food to feed all his helpers on Christmas Day. He knows Mrs Christmas needs time to cook the food, so he instructs Rudolph to go to the supermarket and buy everything they need. The list is long and Rudolph has divided the list between his friends so they can find the food quickly, but now they can't find each other. Can you help?

- [ ] A can of baked beans
- [ ] A gnome
- [ ] A blue bag
- [ ] An elf reading a book
- [ ] A black and white cat
- [ ] A red pram
- [ ] A boy sucking his thumb
- [ ] A woman with a broken arm
- [ ] An alien
- [ ] A man carrying 5 shopping bags

BAKERY

Market Madness

As a special treat, Rudolph and his friends have taken their sleigh to Germany to buy some Christmas stocking fillers at the German market. They can't let the girls and boys see them. Can you find them and make sure they get back to Father Christmas's workshop in one piece?

- [ ] A girl in an orange dress
- [ ] A boy in green lederhosen
- [ ] The German flag
- [ ] A suitcase
- [ ] 10 sausages
- [ ] A snow globe
- [ ] Someone looking at a map
- [ ] An owl
- [ ] A baseball cap
- [ ] A lady wearing sunglasses

Mrs Christmas's Kitchen

Now Rudolph has been shopping in the supermarket, Mrs Christmas has all the food she needs. She has decided to bake some mince pies and cook the turkey. Noelle and her elves have offered to help Mrs Christmas, and so have Rudolph, Rocky, Blue, Marvin and Father Christmas. Suddenly, the kitchen is very busy!

- [ ] A carton of milk
- [ ] An elf in a tutu
- [ ] A wizard's hat
- [ ] An elf with his hair on fire
- [ ] Headphones
- [ ] A ginger cat
- [ ] A penguin pulling a cracker
- [ ] A rocking horse
- [ ] 10 carrots
- [ ] A radio

Let it Snow

After all that baking, some of Rudolph's festive helpers have decided to enjoy the snow, including Rocky, who is keen to practise his moves on the slopes! They shouldn't stay out too late, though, because they promised Father Christmas they would clean the sleigh in the afternoon.

- [ ] Yellow skates
- [ ] Brown bear skiing
- [ ] A reindeer wearing sunglasses
- [ ] A yeti
- [ ] Someone with a broken leg
- [ ] A snowboarder
- [ ] A fur hat
- [ ] A woman in a bikini
- [ ] 10 rabbits
- [ ] A girl wearing a pink ski jacket

On Ice

Uh-oh, Rudolph was having such a good time that he forgot he was Father Christmas's second in command. Instead, he decided to go ice-skating with Rocky and their friends. Father Christmas isn't very happy and has gone to find them. Can you round them all up before Father Christmas does?

- [ ] A man in shorts
- [ ] A rag doll
- [ ] A daffodil
- [ ] 12 blue scarves
- [ ] A pink tree
- [ ] A boy blowing his nose
- [ ] A green snowflake
- [ ] A bunch of holly
- [ ] An igloo
- [ ] An Eskimo

Reindeer Training School

Rudolph is trying to be a good reindeer today. He is teaching the other reindeer how to be the best they can be. If they want to make the elite flying squad, they are going to have to work very hard. Rocky, Blue, Noelle, Marvin and Father Christmas have decided to join in because, although it is hard work, it's a lot of fun!

- ☐ A flying penguin
- ☐ A yellow hula-hoop
- ☐ 5 purple balls
- ☐ A red slide
- ☐ A donkey
- ☐ A man in army clothes
- ☐ A reindeer wearing glasses
- ☐ A broken sledge
- ☐ 10 red cones
- ☐ A whistle

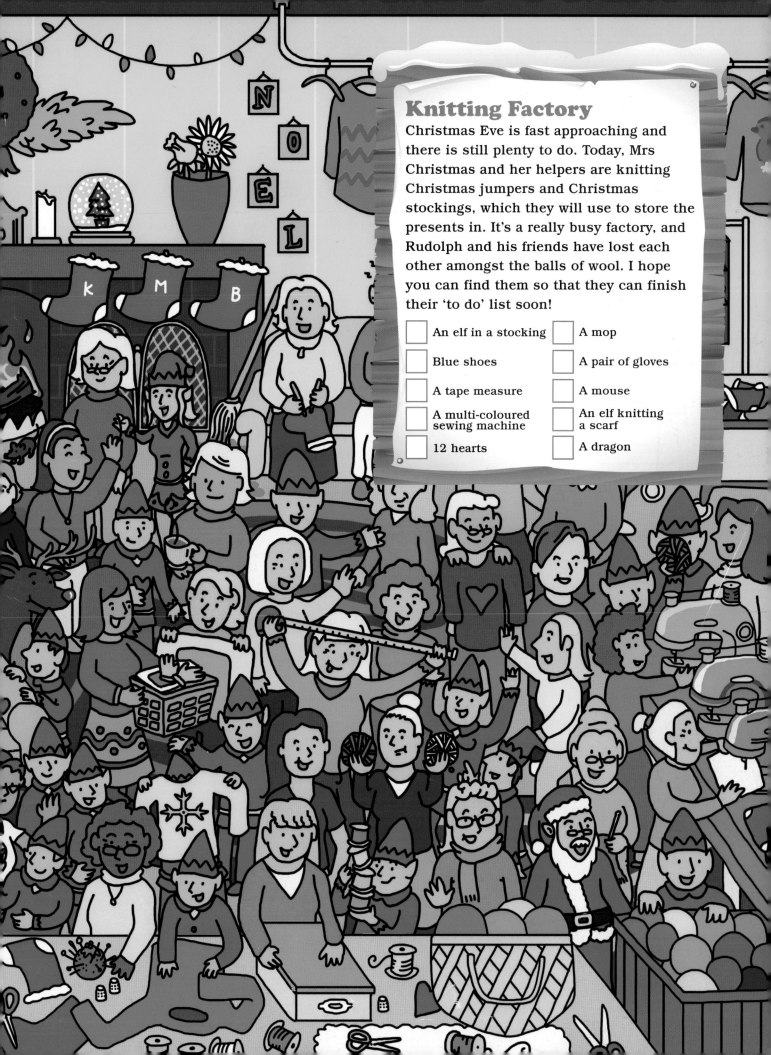

Knitting Factory

Christmas Eve is fast approaching and there is still plenty to do. Today, Mrs Christmas and her helpers are knitting Christmas jumpers and Christmas stockings, which they will use to store the presents in. It's a really busy factory, and Rudolph and his friends have lost each other amongst the balls of wool. I hope you can find them so that they can finish their 'to do' list soon!

- [ ] An elf in a stocking
- [ ] Blue shoes
- [ ] A tape measure
- [ ] A multi-coloured sewing machine
- [ ] 12 hearts
- [ ] A mop
- [ ] A pair of gloves
- [ ] A mouse
- [ ] An elf knitting a scarf
- [ ] A dragon

Elf Workshop

Rudolph and his friends have swapped the knitting factory for the elf workshop. It's time to start putting the presents in the knitted stocking. Noelle is worried because the elves haven't finished making the presents yet. Everyone is going to have to work very hard today, especially if they want all the good girls and boys to receive their presents. Help Rudolph find his friends so that he can give them instructions to help them work quicker.

- [ ] A pair of roller skates
- [ ] A sack of coal
- [ ] A toy train
- [ ] An elf wrapped in blue paper
- [ ] A zebra
- [ ] Spotty wrapping paper
- [ ] 10 name tags
- [ ] A dolls pram
- [ ] A red and yellow stocking
- [ ] A pink sock

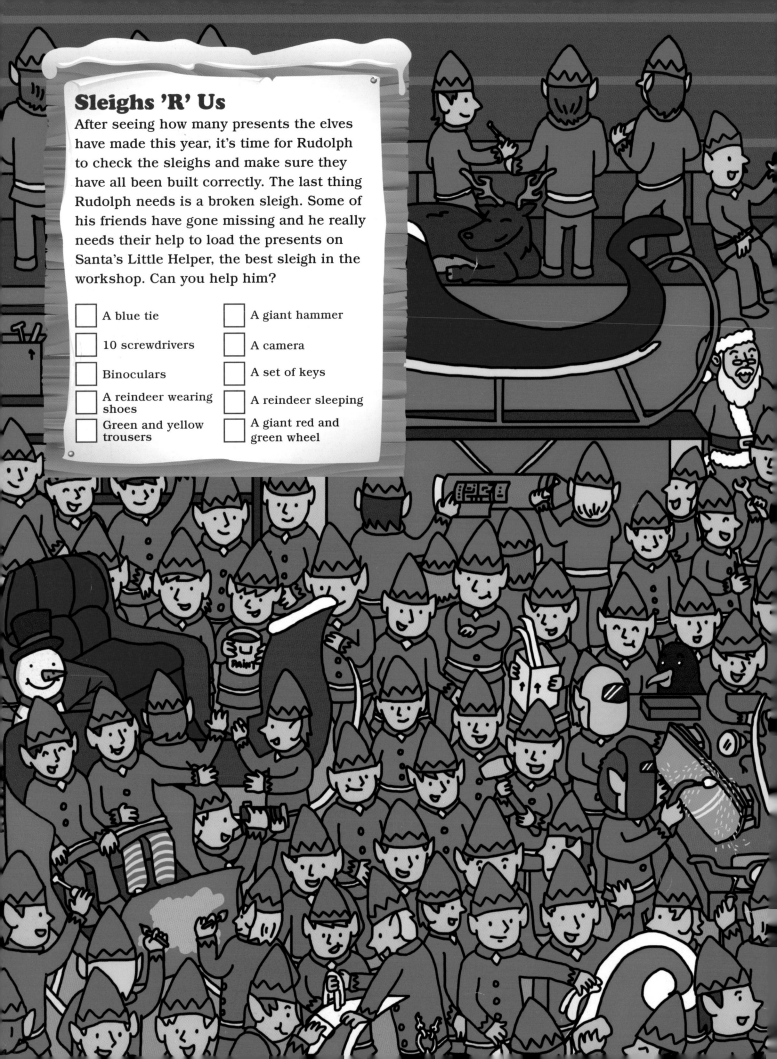

Sleighs 'R' Us

After seeing how many presents the elves have made this year, it's time for Rudolph to check the sleighs and make sure they have all been built correctly. The last thing Rudolph needs is a broken sleigh. Some of his friends have gone missing and he really needs their help to load the presents on Santa's Little Helper, the best sleigh in the workshop. Can you help him?

- [ ] A blue tie
- [ ] 10 screwdrivers
- [ ] Binoculars
- [ ] A reindeer wearing shoes
- [ ] Green and yellow trousers
- [ ] A giant hammer
- [ ] A camera
- [ ] A set of keys
- [ ] A reindeer sleeping
- [ ] A giant red and green wheel

Blizzard

Christmas Eve has finally arrived and Rudolph and his festive helper are checking everything on the list has been achieved. Thankfully, Rudolph has done a fantastic job, and so have you and his friends! Father Christmas is a little worried because there is a blizzard, but this only makes Rudolph more excited. He loves flying in the blizzard because he can see through the snow, and he loves the cold wind in his fur. Can you help him locate his friends, who aren't as good at seeing in the blizzard?

- [ ] A troll
- [ ] 5 snowmen
- [ ] A bike
- [ ] 5 penguins in blue scarves
- [ ] A blue and green bauble
- [ ] 5 giant snowflakes
- [ ] The North Star
- [ ] 5 reindeer wearing hats
- [ ] A teddy bear
- [ ] A skateboard

It's Christmas...

After a fantastic take-off, Rudolph has done a brilliant job delivering presents all around the world. Now they have carefully landed in London and started to hand out the presents. Can you count the number of presents they have delivered?

Add them all up and put your answer here.

Travel London!

Answers

Did you spot Father Christmas's hidden present he wrapped just for you? Go back through the illustrations and look for it! If you can't find the present, it's circled in the answers below.

Toyshop

Mail Mania

Tree Maze

A Christmas Carol

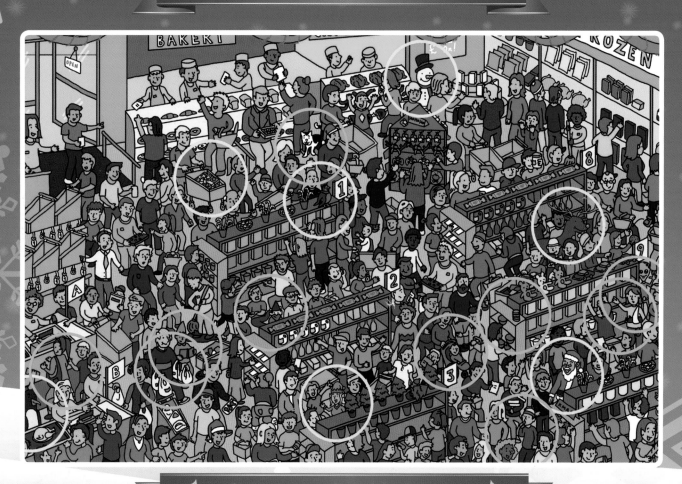

Supermarket Madness

Market Madness

Mrs Christmas's Kitchen

Let it Snow

On Ice

Reindeer Training School

Knitting Factory

Elf Workshop

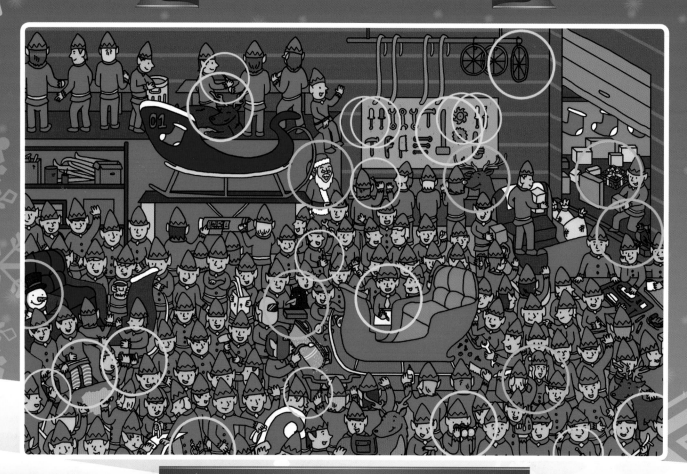

Sleighs 'R' Us

Blizzard

Answer =19

Travel London!

It's Christmas...

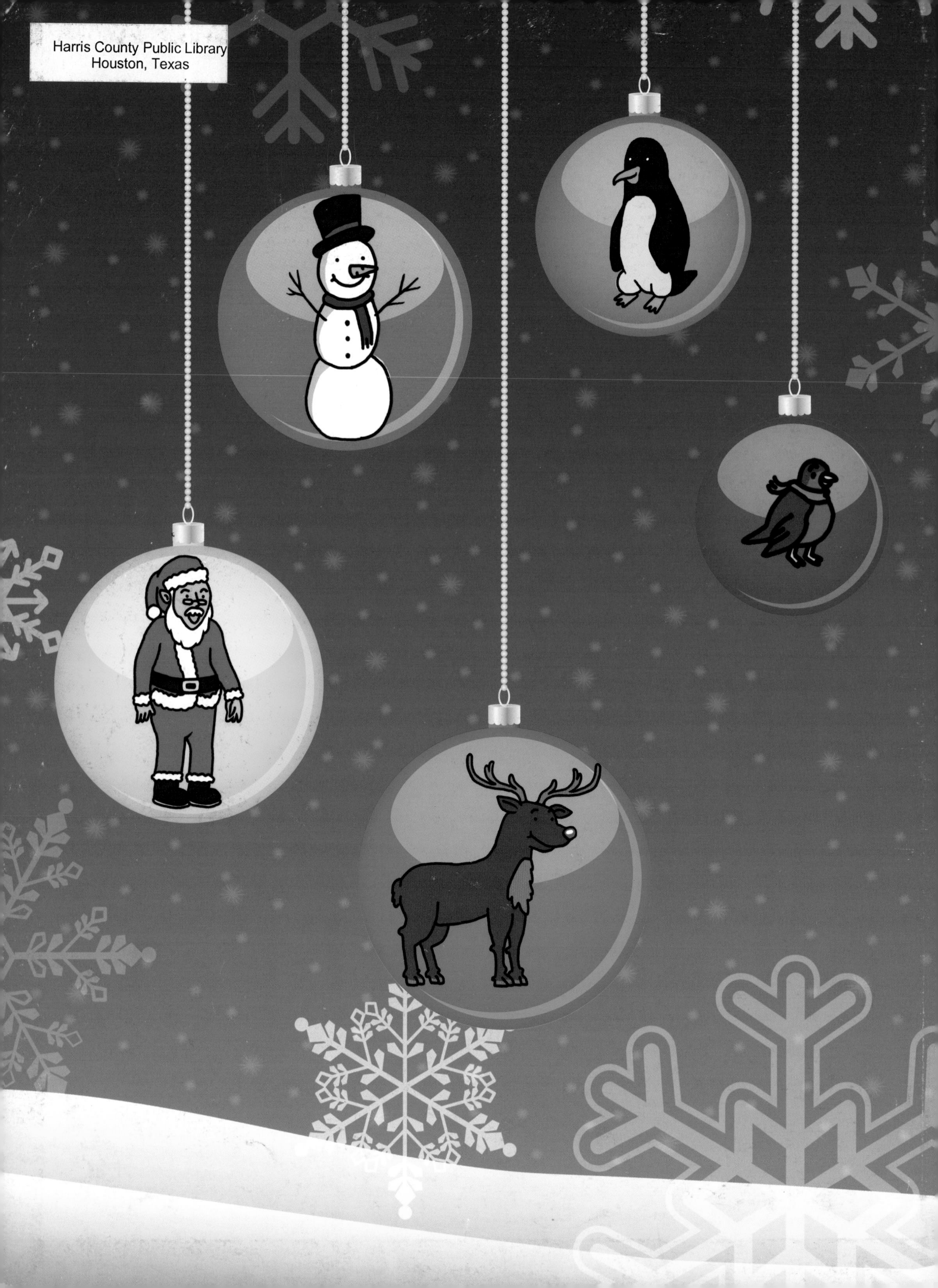